Contents

 Fiction

Tremor
page 2

Non-fiction

Earthquakes
page 18

Written by
Diana Bentley
Sylvia Karavis
Illustrated by
Peter Richardson

Series editor **Dee Reid**

T0351692

P Pearson

Characters

Agent Em

Agent Vee

Agent Que

Agent Zed

Tremor

Tricky words

- suddenly
- crackled
- appeared
- shock-waves
- thousands
- centre
- huge
- destroy

Read these words to the student. Help them with these words when they appear in the text

Introduction

The four agents were in their Base when suddenly all the alarms went off and an evil face appeared on their screen. It is Tremor, the super-villain, whose shock-waves have made huge cracks around the world and killed thousands of people. She plans to kill the agents too, if they try to stop her. Zed has a plan but will the blaster stop Tremor?

Tremor

The agents were in the Base when suddenly the alarms went off.

Just then the blank screen crackled into life and an evil face appeared.

"I am Tremor.
I have made huge cracks around the world with my shock-waves.
Thousands of people have been killed.
I will kill you too, if you try to stop me."

Then the screen went blank.

4

"We have to stop her," said Em. "But how can we fight her shock-waves?"

"We can't fight her shock-waves," said Zed. "But I have a plan. We can use the blaster to stop her."

"How?" said Que.

But just then the Base began to shake and a crack appeared in the floor.

The agents ran outside.
There was Tremor.
There were cracks in the ground around her.

"Ready for a trip to the centre of the earth?" she said.
She raised her hand and shot a shock-wave towards the agents.

8

The waves hit the ground.
The ground began to shake and
another huge crack appeared.

The ground began to shake and the agents began to slip closer and closer towards the crack.
Tremor shot another shock-wave at the agents.

The wave hit Vee and she began to slip into the crack.

Just in time Em grabbed her hair and pulled her back.

"Time to fight back!" said Que.
Em and Zed shot the blaster at
the ground around Tremor.
A huge crack appeared.

Tremor laughed, "You idiots, you think you can fight me!" and she ran at them.

As she ran, they shot the blaster at the crack again.
The crack got bigger and bigger.

Tremor tried to shoot but it was too late.
She slipped and fell down into the huge crack.

"She won't be back for a long time," said Que.

"Just as well," said Vee. "I didn't fancy a trip to the centre of the earth!"

"Tremor is gone for now," said Zed. "But others will try to destroy the world. We must be ready for them."

Quiz ////////////////////////

Text comprehension

Literal comprehension
p11 How did Em save Vee?
p12 How did the agents get rid of Tremor?

Inferential comprehension
p4 How do you know Tremor is evil?
p8 Why does Tremor try to joke with the agents?
p12 How can you tell the agents are feeling brave?

Personal response
- Do you think Zed's plan was clever?
- Do you think Tremor might come back?

Word knowledge

p6 Find a word that rhymes with 'make'.
p7 What are the actual words spoken?
p11 Find two past tense verbs ending in 'ed'.

Spelling challenge

Read these words:

tried   walk   never

Now try to spell them!

Ha! Ha! Ha!

What did the ground say to the earthquake?

You crack me up!

Find out about

- how an earthquake came without warning and destroyed the capital city of Haiti.

Tricky words

- earthquake
- suddenly
- damage
- building
- destroyed
- sewage
- emergency
- vehicles

Read these words to the student. Help them with these words when they appear in the text.

Introduction

Earthquakes come without warning and cause terrible damage. In January 2010 an earthquake hit the capital city of Haiti. Thousands of people died and the city was destroyed. Emergency vehicles couldn't get help to the trapped people because the roads had cracked wide open.

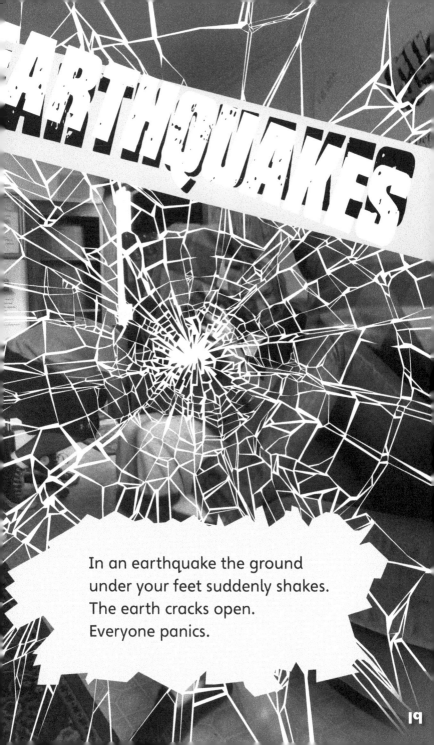

EARTHQUAKES

In an earthquake the ground under your feet suddenly shakes. The earth cracks open. Everyone panics.

What is it like in an earthquake?

Earthquakes hit without warning and
cause terrible damage.
Houses fall down and some
people get trapped.

Roads crack wide open.
People who go outside get
hit by glass and bricks.
In an earthquake many
people get hurt.

What to do in an earthquake

Don't panic!
If you are inside:
Get under a table.
Cover your head with your hands.
Don't go outside.
Wait for help to get to you.

If you are outside:
Stop your car.
Go inside a building.
Don't go near walls or trees,
they might fall on you.

Earthquake in Haiti

On 12th January 2010 an earthquake hit Haiti.
Suddenly the earth began to shake.
The roads began to crack wide open.

The earthquake lasted around 30 seconds and the capital city of Haiti was destroyed. Houses fell down and thousands of people were trapped.
People ran into the streets but were hit by glass and bricks.

People who had not been hurt tried to help.
They used their hands to try to get to
people trapped under the buildings.

Dust filled the air.
It was difficult to see or breathe.
Sewage pipes had cracked and sewage
ran over the roads.

No emergency vehicles could get to the people because the roads had cracked. No-one could get through to lift the bricks off the trapped people.

News of the terrible earthquake
went around the world.
Everyone wanted to help.
Many people gave money.
Some people wanted to go and help
but the airport was destroyed.
It took days for help to get to Haiti.

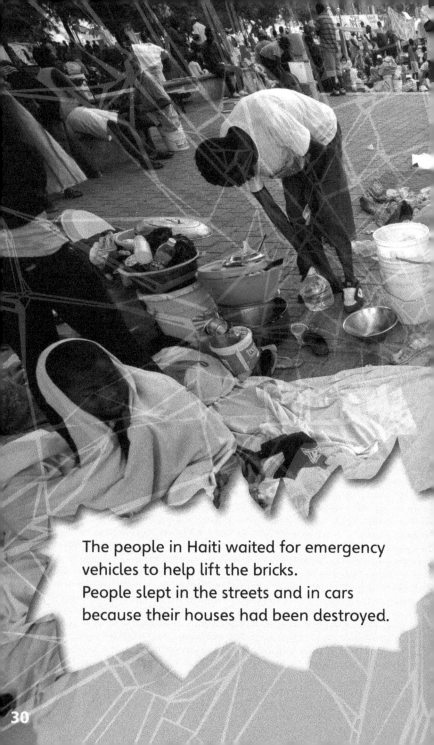

The people in Haiti waited for emergency vehicles to help lift the bricks.
People slept in the streets and in cars because their houses had been destroyed.

Over 200,000 people died in the earthquake and over 2 million people had their houses destroyed.
Some help has got to Haiti now but over 1 million people are still living in tents.

Quiz ///////////////

Text comprehension

Literal comprehension
p24 When did the earthquake hit Haiti?

p28 Why couldn't emergency vehicles get through to help people?

Inferential comprehension
p19 Why do people panic in an earthquake?

p27 Why do people often get sick after there has been an earthquake?

p30 Did the people of Haiti get all the help they needed?

Personal response
- What do you think would be the scariest thing about being in an earthquake?
- Would you rather risk being hit by glass or trapped in a building?

Word knowledge

p22 Which two words are combined in the word 'Don't'?

p25 Find a word meaning 'ruined'.

p28 Which connective joins the two parts of the first sentence?

Spelling challenge

Read these words:

over   any   last

Now try to spell them!

Ha! Ha! Ha!

What happens to cows during an earthquake?

They give milk shakes!